Best School Jokes Ever

Matt Rissinger & Philip Yates
Illustrated by Jeff Sinclair

Sterling Publishing Co., Inc.
New York

To my daughters—Rebecca, Emily, and Abigail.—M.R.

To the Pine Street Gang—Patty, Bill, Matthew, Billy, and Parick McCann—and in loving memory of Pavel and Phil, the guinea pigs.—P.Y.

Library of Congress Cataloguing-in-Publication Data

Rissinger, Matt.
    Best school jokes ever / Matt Rissinger & Philip Yates ; illustrated by Jeff Sinclair.
        p.   cm.
    Includes index.
    Summary: A collection of jokes, riddles, one-liners, and other forms of humor related to classes, homework, field trips, and other aspects of school.
    ISBN 0-8069-9869-5
    1. Schools—Juvenile humor. 2. Education—Juvenile humor. 3. Wit and humor, Juvenile. [1. Schools—Wit and humor. 2. Jokes.] I. Yates, Philip, 1956-   . II. Sinclair, Jeff, ill. III. Title.
    PN6231.S3R57 1998
    371'.002'07—dc21   97-50481
                                                        CIP
                                                        AC

10 9 8 7 6 5 4 3 2 1

Published by Sterling Publishing Company, Inc.
387 Park Avenue South, New York, N.Y. 10016
© 1998 by Philip Yates and Matt Rissinger
Illustrations © 1998 by Jeff Sinclair
Distributed in Canada by Sterling Publishing
℅ Canadian Manda Group, One Atlantic Avenue, Suite 105
Toronto, Ontario, Canada M6K 3E7
Distributed in Great Britain and Europe by Cassell PLC
Wellington House, 125 Strand, London WC2R 0BB, England
Distributed in Australia by Capricorn Link (Australia) Pty Ltd.
P.O. Box 6651, Baulkham Hills, Business Centre, NSW 2153, Australia
Manufactured in the United States of America
All rights reserved

Sterling ISBN 0-8069-9869-5

Contents

1. CLASS CLOWNING AROUND

SLUSH!!!

TEACHER: If you misbehave again, I'll have to teach you a lesson.
CLASS CLOWN: Hooray, I'm finally going to learn something!

TEACHER: Today we're going to watch a video about the history of medicine.
HUMPHREY: Oh, please, not another doc-umentary.

KOOKY COURSES

JAKE: How are you doing in wood-carving class?
DRAKE: I'm getting better whittle by whittle.

LANA: How did you like needlecraft?
DANA: I liked it up to a point.

MINDY: Did you like that course you took in decision making?
CINDY: Yes and no.

FUNNY FIELD TRIPS

SCIENCE TEACHER: Well, class, are you looking forward to our field trip to the national tree museum?
CLASS CLOWN: Personally, I can take it or leaf it.

DAD: Hey, Danny, why aren't you going on the field trip to the Mint?
DAN: Somehow it doesn't make a lot of cents to me.

THE CLASS CLOWN'S READING LIST

How to Behave in the Classroom,
by Sid Down and Bea Quiet

My Favorite Time of the Day,
by Belle Rings and Rhea Cess

How I Became a Genius, by Skip A. Grade

The Book of Confusion, by Kay Oss Rains

DAFFY DEFINITIONS

Tomorrow–The time when most students
like to do their homework.
Homework–An activity performed
in between video games.
Sleep–The perfect exercise when school
lets out for the summer.

A teacher called the mother of one her students to complain.

"I have bad news and good news about your son Johnny. The bad news is he's the worst-behaved child in my class!"

"What's the good news?" asked Johnny's mother.

"The good news is he has perfect attendance!"

What do dragons like most about school?
The fire drills.

One day the school troublemaker was sent to the
principal's office.

"Do you know why you're here?" asked the
principal.

"Is it about this morning?" asked the
troublemaker.

"Your teacher says you ran in the hall, beat up two
students, started a food fight in the cafeteria, and
cursed at one of your classmates."

"Boy, that's a relief," sighed the troublemaker. "I
thought maybe you found out I broke your
windshield."

What did the wad of gum say to the school desk?
"I'm stuck on you!"

Our school is so old-fashioned the clock in our classroom is a sundial.

One day Hubert gave his speech to the class.
"There's too much violence on television," he began. "I watched TV the other day and there were six murders, three fist fights, two earthquakes, and a nuclear disaster. I swear, that's the last time I get up early to watch Saturday morning cartoons."

The kids at our school have their own cellular phones. When the teacher wants them to figure out a problem, she really does call them to the blackboard.

Where do ghosts go when the dismissal bell rings?
To the after-ghoul program.

When the third-grade class went on a field trip to the circus, two boys broke away from the rest of the group and decided to look around. Before long, they came upon a trailer with a sign saying, "The Smallest Man in the World." Knocking on the door, they were astonished when a man nearly eight feet tall appeared on the doorstep.
"Isn't this the home of the World's Smallest Man?" asked the first boy.
"Yes," replied the giant. "But I'm afraid you caught me on my day off."

VIDEOS FROM THE SELF-HELP SHELF

Powerful Microscope, hosted by Seymour Cells

Defending Yourself in the Courtroom,
hosted by Iris Mye Case

Safe River Crossing, hosted by Jethro D. Bote

Home Demolition, hosted by Wallace Falling

Curing Hunger Pangs, hosted by Aida Bigg Snacke

TV Alternatives, hosted by Rita Goode Booke

Solving Crimes, hosted by Anita Clew

Protecting Your Valuables, hosted by Jules R. Missing

How to Make Leather Crafts, hosted by Tanya Hide

Giving Class Assembly Speeches,
hosted by Audie Torium

How to Sleep in Class While the Teacher Gives Notes,
hosted by Chuck Bored

How did the trombone manage to pass first grade?
The teacher let it slide.

10

What's gray and dusty and goes "Cough-cough!"
An elephant cleaning erasers.

Knock-knock!
 Who's there?
Dismissal.
 Dismissal who?
Dismissal will never fire!

TEACHER: Dana, use the word "harmony" in a
 sentence.
DANA: Harmony more jokes like these can a person
 take?

2. READING, WRITING & RIDICULOUS

One of the kids in my English class is so dumb he thinks a prefix is what you do before you break something.

TEACHER: Stacy, read the class your sentence.
STACY: "I don't have no friends."
TEACHER: No. "I don't have any friends. I don't have any friends."
STACY: Gee, Teacher, no wonder you're so unhappy.

What are a gambler's favorite vowels?
I-O-U.

NED: I'm reading a book that shows you how to build storage spaces.
ED: Oh, one of those shelf-help books.

GRAMMAR GUFFAWS

TEACHER: Stu, please use the word "camphor" in a sentence.
STU: Next summer my parents are sending me to camphor a week.

TEACHER: Jerry, please use the word "acquire" in a sentence.
JERRY: Someday I want to sing in acquire.

TEACHER: Janey, use the words "depart," "decide," and "deface" in a sentence.
JANEY: Depart of your hair should never hang over decide of deface.

Did you hear about the new magazine in the library for athletic dogs? It's called "Spots Illustrated."

Did you hear about the baker who wrote a mystery novel? It's a real who-donut.

How do librarians catch fish?
With bookworms.

REQUIRED READING LIST

Ketchup Recipes, by Tom Mato

How to Stay Tidy, by Colleen Thea House

Strong Man, by Jim Nasium

I Ran the Boston Marathon, by Emma I. Tired

Blowout, by Aaron D. Tires

I'm Sorry, You're Sorry, by A. Paula Jize

My Life as a Landscaper, by Moe Grass

The Wrong Man, by Hans Offme

Camera Techniques, by Otto Focus

Gas Guzzler, by Phil Mye Tank

Nuclear Power, by Ray D. Ashun

What is a dog's favorite book of stories?
Canterbury Tails.

A crook rushed into a library and pointed a gun at the clerk.

"This is a stickup!" said the crook.

"Can't you see that sign?" said the librarian in a whisper. "It says no loud noises in the library."

"Don't worry, " the crook reassured her, "I'm using a silencer."

What would you get if you crossed a famous children's book author with a Greek god?
Dr. Zeus.

TEACHER: How did Webster invent the dictionary?
HELEN: He got into an argument and one word led to another.

Did you hear about the silkworm who became a story teller? She sits around all day and spins yarns.

What author wrote mysteries about fried chicken?
Agatha Crispy.

WHERE CAN I FIND...?

BOY: Where can I find the book *Boys Are Smarter Than Girls*?
LIBRARIAN: Try the fiction shelf.

"Can I check out this book on blood clots?"
  "Sorry, that doesn't circulate."

"Where can I find a book called *Life in the Convent?*"
  "That would be in nun-fiction."

LIBRARIAN: Why is this book you returned all wet?
JOHNNY: I left it out on the lawn last night.
LIBRARIAN: I'm afraid it's way over-dew.

Mr. Harper, the English teacher, asked Mary to give him a sentence with an object.
  "You are very handsome," replied Mary.
  "Good," said Mr. Harper, "but what is the object?"
  "To get an A in English," said Mary.

GENE: How am I supposed to write a five-page essay about my brain?
IRENE: Easy, just hand in five blank pieces of paper.

Knock-knock!
  Who's there?
Unaware.
  Unaware who?
Unaware is what you put on before your pants.

DUMB DEFINITION

Jungle Gym—Tarzan's younger brother.

What did the lamb like best about its computer?
It was ewe-ser friendly.

TEACHER: Homer, did you the finish reading *The
  History of Milk*?
HOMER: No, but I skimmed most of it.

TEACHER: Did you finish reading the book on
  jungle animals?
FLOYD: To be honest, I read between the lions.

TEACHER: Can you define "procrastination"?
GOMER: Yes, but not right now.

If Samuel Clemens had cloned himself, we would have identical Twains.

What do word lovers eat for breakfast?
   Scrabbled eggs.

DEREK: I bought a book called *How to Handle Disappointment.*
ERIC: Was it helpful?
DEREK: When I opened it, the pages were empty.

JACK: Hey, Mom, I learned five new letters today!
MOM: Oh, yes? Which ones?
JACK: F-L-U-N-K.

3. GYM DANDIES

MICKEY: Why are fish such terrible tennis players?
RICKY: They're afraid to get too close to the net.

What do you call a basketball player who's always on the sidelines?
  Hoop-less.

What has four wheels and can knock down a hundred pins at once?
  A bowl-dozer.

DAD: Hey, son, I heard you went out for the football team?

CHAD: Right. The coach sent me out to buy pizza.

DON: Why did the volleyball players want Stegosaurus on its team?

JON: Because he was a good spiker.

What would you get if you crossed nursery rhymes with yogis?

Mother Gurus.

HIKER #1: Look, the signs says "Waterfall—Five Miles."

HIKER #2: Wow, that's pretty big!

When it looked like they were losing badly, the soccer coach in desperation jumped up and pointed to his worst player. "Henry," he said, " I want you to go out there and get mean and ugly!"

"Whatever you say, Coach!" replied Henry.

Springing to his feet, Henry looked over the other team players. "Hey, Coach?" he said, "which one's Mean and which one's Ugly?"

CHRISSIE: My dad can swim, jump rope, play football, basketball, horseshoes, can sky dive and ski.
MISSIE: He sounds like a jock-of-all-trades.

What would you get if you crossed basketball and a sidewalk game?
Hoopscotch.

Why did the basketball coach suspend the kangaroo?
It kept jumping out of bounds.

ANDY: Did you hear the basketball game was postponed on account of rain?
SANDY: I guess they were afraid of double-dribbling.

FLIP: What beverage helps boxers count?
FLOP: A one-two punch.

Why did the bungee jumper go the plastic surgeon?
To get rid of her stretch marks.

What did the scale say to the dieter?
"You have a weigh to go."

PLAY BALL!

NED: What position did the dairy farmer play on the football team?
FRED: Half and halfback.

STEVE: What position did the marine play on the baseball team?
REEVE: "Right, left, right, left field."

VIDEOS FROM THE FITNESS SHELF

The Dangers of Running, hosted by Belle E. Cramps

Aerobics,
hosted by Stan Upp, Sid Down, and Ben Dover

Swimming Tips, hosted by Doug E. Paddle

Who's the top player on the jungle football team?
The lion backer.

What do robins do before a long-distance race?
They worm up.

What would you get if you crossed a Middle Eastern dish with a toboggan?
Shish kebob-sled.

What chocolate bar can do a hundred sit-ups?
Nestle's Crunch.

Sign at Fencing School: "Out to lunge."

Did you hear about the two furniture polishers who had a contest to see who was faster? It was a race to the finish.

ZIP: Where can you watch chickens race cars?
ZAP: At the Kentucky Fried Derby.

CLINT: Do you know what I love best about baseball?
FLINT: What?
CLINT: The grass and the dirt, the lump in the throat.
FLINT: Yeah, and that's just the hot dogs.

What dinosaur always came in third at Olympic events?

Bronze-tosaurus.

ALL HANDS ON DECK!

What's King Tut's favorite card game?
Gin Mummy.

What is an eel's favorite card game?
Glow Fish!

What card game do fish play by themselves?
Sole-itaire.

Where do golfers keep their equipment?
In tee bags.

Knock-knock!
  Who's there?
Rugby.
  Rugby who?
Rugby fine if you ever vacuumed it.

Two men at the race track were discussing their luck.
  "An amazing thing happened to me the last time I was here," said the first man. "It was the ninth day of the month, and it was the day of my son's ninth birthday. The address of our house was 999, and I arrived here at the track at nine minutes past nine in the morning."
  "I bet you put money on the ninth horse on the card," said the second man.
  "Yes, I did," said the first man.
  "And it won?"
  "No, it came in ninth."

What would you get if you crossed a baseball player with a frog?
An outfielder who catches flies and then eats them.

RHONDA: Where do all the basketball players go when the season's over?
YOLANDA: They go to the movies and sit in the front row.

DIET DILLIES

PHIL: Did you lose weight on the peanut butter diet?

JILL: Not yet, but I think I'll stick with it.

JON: How's that snake diet going?

DON: Shed a few pounds already.

CHRISSIE: I went on two diets.

MISSIE: Why two?

CHRISSIE: Because one diet wasn't giving me enough food.

Who is the feline world heavyweight champion?
Muhammad Alley-cat.

Why was the dog caddy kicked off the golf course?
For barking up the wrong tee.

What do tennis players and lawyers have in common?
Sooner or later, they both have their day in court.

How do they carry injured baseball players off the field?
With a seventh inning stretcher.

"Coach, I want to be a basketball player in the worst way."

"Don't worry, you'll make it."

What do you call a 100-year-old cheerleader?
Old Yeller.

DINA: It cost me $300 to join the gym and I haven't
  lost a pound.
SELENA: Maybe you should try showing up.

What do you get when you cross Arnold
Schwarzenegger with a military weapon?
  A guided muscle.

IGGY: What are Luke Skywalker's favorite baseball
  movies?
ZIGGY: "All-Star Wars" and "The Umpire Strikes
  Back."

4. MATH MIRTH

TEACHER: Define absolute zero.
HENRY: The lowest grade you can get on a test.

TEACHER: What is the equivalent of 60 seconds or
one sixtieth of an hour?
SALLY: Give me a minute and I'll think of it.

TEACHER: Define "infinity."
LARS: Uh, let me see...
TEACHER: Go ahead, guess.
LARS: Uh, uh...
TEACHER: Come on, you can do it.
LARS: This could take forever.
TEACHER: Forever is correct!

TEACHER: What do we mean when we say "estimate"?

SUZY: Can I guess?

TEACHER: Guess is correct.

Why did the fraction go on a diet?
It was trying to reduce.

What do math teachers take for a cold?
Alka-Seltzer Plus.

What do you call eight woodcutters in pajamas?
A lumber party.

REQUIRED MATH BOOKS

Math Made Easy, by Cal Q. Later

Straight Lines, by Ray D. Uss

Super Subtraction, by Carry D. Wun

Arithmetic Problems, by Betty Kant Add

"Dad, if 50 antelope are grazing on the plain and 75 more join them, how many antelope are there altogether?"
"Boy, I hate that gnu math."

What is a hunter's favorite subject?
Trigger-nometry.

What do math teachers enjoy with their coffee?
A slice of pi.

TEACHER: If you ran 1,093 yards on Tuesday, then ran the same distance on Wednesday, what would you get?

RAMA: Exhausted.

DOWN FOR THE COUNT

TEACHER: Can you count to 10?

DAVID: Yes, teacher. (counting on his fingers) One, two, three, four, five, six, seven, eight, nine, ten.

TEACHER: Very good. Now this time count on your head.

DAVID: Yes, teacher. (He stands on his head and counts) One, two, three, four, five, six, seven, eight, nine, ten.

What numbers are always wandering?
Roamin' numerals.

Did you hear about the dumbest crook in the world? He kidnapped identical twins, then demanded $900,000 or $500,000 apiece.

How is an overweight person like a kid failing math?
They both need help with their figures.

Knock-knock!
  Who's there?
Canoe.
  Canoe who?
Canoe help me with my math problems?

Knock-knock!
  Who's there?
Imus.
  Imus who?
Imus get an "A" on my math test.

What was the butterfly's favorite class?
  Moth-ematics.

DAD: Did you pass algebra?
TOM: I sure did.
DAD: Then what is this "F" on your report card?
TOM: Because every time I came to school I passed right by algebra class.

What would you get if you crossed a hootenanny with a math class?

Square root dancing.

Did you hear about the dumbest mathematician in the world? He bought a pocket calculator so he could figure out how many pockets he owned.

TEACHER: If there are 365 days in the year, and 24 hours in a day, how many seconds are there?

DONALD: Twelve.

TEACHER: How do you figure that?

DONALD: Well, there's January second, then February second, then March second....

MUTT: I just bought a super-quick computer to do my math homework for me.

JEFF: But you don't even know how to work the old one.

MUTT: True, but now I can make the same mistakes twice as fast.

TEACHER: Carol, use the word "centimeter" in a sentence.

CAROL: When my aunt arrived at the airport my dad was centimeter.

5. JEST TESTING!

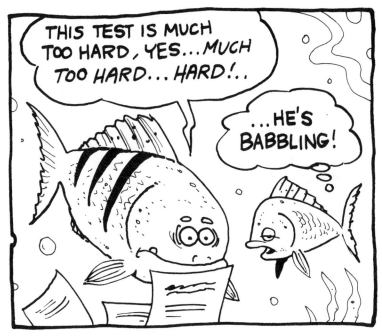

What kind of tests are fish good at?
Open brook tests.

What do skeletons do before a big test?
They bone up.

Why was the sheep grounded?
He brought home a baaa-d report card.

What kind of tests are dentists good at?
True or floss.

TEACHER: Randy, did I catch you just now copying Alan's test paper?

RANDY: No way, I haven't copied his paper for 10 minutes.

DAFFY DEFINITION

Magic Marker—A magician who grades papers.

GRADE GIGGLES

What two letters would you find on a musician's report card?

C-D.

What three letters on a report card will help you get home?

C-A-B.

What three letters on a report card will never last?

F-A-D.

"Son, the reason you're getting bad grades is that you spend too much time watching game shows."

"I'm sorry, Dad, but you'll have to phrase that in the form of a question."

FREDDY: My teacher grades like she drives.

TEDDY: How's that?

FREDDY: She never uses the passing lane.

What happened to the composer who failed all his subjects?

He was held Bach a year.

Why do witches always do well on the computer?

They use a spell checker.

HOW DID THEY GRADUATE?

The hot dog made the honor roll.

The boat earned a sculler-ship.

The flower got all bees.

The plankton graduated on the bottom.

What grades did the Neanderthal man get on his report card?

B.C.

When do mummies do well in school?

When they get all wrapped up in their studies.

MOM: Your teacher says you flunked swimming.

CHRIS: I couldn't stay afloat.

MOM: I think you've sunk to a new low.

DAD: If you passed your exam, why did the teacher fail you?

CHAD: Because I passed it to the kid next to me.

TEACHER: Chris, are you copying Larry's paper?
CHRIS: What gave me away? Was it the binoculars?

TEACHER: Quick, class, who can spell "collie"?
HAROLD: Is this another one of those pup quizzes?

TEACHER: What is aftermath?
DANA: The feeling you get when you finish an
    arithmetic test.

What did the circle say to the triangle?
    "I'll be around if you need me!"

"Vince, spell snake."
    "S-N-A-K."
"What's at the end of it?"
    "A rattle."

"Shelby, spell doctor."
    "D-O-C-T-O."
"What comes next?"
    "Usually, the bill."

What is the difference between an optometrist and
a teacher grading tests?
    One examines your eyes, the other eyes your exams.

BENNY: What's big and gray and takes the bus
everywhere?
LENNY: An elephant that failed its driver's test.

SILLY SENTENCES

TEACHER: Roddy, use "ransom" in a sentence.
RODDY: Yesterday afternoon I walked some, then I
ransom.

TEACHER: Manuel, define "ignorance" and
"apathy."
MANUEL: I don't know and I don't care.
TEACHER: Yes, that's correct.

TEACHER: Use "malign" in a sentence.
BILLY: I sure hope a fish bites malign.

TEACHER: Can anyone use "finite" in a sentence?
MIGUEL: I can. It's a finite for a walk in the park.

TEACHER: Dana, use the word "vertigo" in a
sentence.
DANA: On my first day of school I was so lost I
didn't know vertigo.

TEACHER: Tod, use the word "migrate" in a
sentence.
TODD: Every Christmas migrate grandfather comes
to visit.

6. IN STITCHES!

Boy to school nurse:
"I dropped my laptop computer in the snow."
  "What do you want me to do?"
  "Treat it for frost-byte."

Little Priscilla went to the school nurse and said,
"My head hurts, my belly hurts, and my arms and
legs hurt."
  After checking the girl over, the nurse pulled out a
tiny hammer and tapped Priscilla's knees to check
her reflexes.
  "How do you feel now?" asked the nurse.
  "Worse!" groaned Priscilla. "Now my knees hurt."

NUTTY NURSE COMEBACKS

SCHOOL NURSE: How did it feel when you hit your finger with the hammer?
DONALD: Smashing!

SCHOOL NURSE: How do you feel after getting hit by a baseball?
BILLY: Never felt batter!

SCHOOL NURSE: Do you have a cold?
BOBBY: No, I'm just rehearsing for the part of Sneezy in *Snow White and the Seven Dwarfs*.

SCHOOL NURSE: Why do you think you're a bird?
DANNY: Never mind, just tweet me.

CLARA: How much did it cost to have your tonsils removed?
SARA: A thousand dollars.
CLARA: Why so much?
SARA: $500 for the operation and $500 for the ice cream.

Boy to school nurse:
"Nurse, nurse, I think a bee crawled inside my ear.
"You seem fine. What gave you that idea?"
"I don't know, but it's been going through my head all day."

LUBY: Do you have a dental plan?
RUBY: Yes, I chew on the other side.

CINDY: I sneezed 300 times today. Do you think there's something in the air?
MINDY: Yes, your germs.

When his mother got sick, Danny decided to cook dinner for her. He boiled noodles, poured sauce over them, and served them to her in bed.

"This is delicious," said his mother. "Did you find the spaghetti strainer okay?"

"No, I didn't," said Danny, "so I used a fly swatter."

"Oh, Danny," his mother gagged, spitting out the noodles, "how could you?"

"Don't worry," said Danny, "I used the old one."

EXCUSES, EXCUSES!

From a hockey player: "My son has a bad case of chicken pucks."

From a car battery salesman: "Please excuse my daughter from school today. She's feeling a bit run down."

From a chimney sweep: "My son won't be in school today. He caught the flue."

From a millionaire architect: "My son will be out for the rest of the year. He's decided to build his own school."

JACK: I don't know whether to be a brain surgeon or a novelist.
MACK: Why don't you flip a coin—heads or tales.

THE WORLD'S DUMBEST EXCUSE NOTE

Dear Mrs. Smith:
 Bobby will be out the rest of the week due to a football injury. He hut-hut-hut himself.

School nurse to sick boy:
"What is your name, so we can notify your parents?"
 "Don't worry, my parents already know my name."

"What do you plan to take for your cold?" the teacher asked Dana.
 "I think I'll take the rest of the week off," said Dana.

PHIL: I hardly felt a thing when the dentist stuck a needle in my cheek.
WILL: Now that's what I call a jab well done.

TEACHER: Lenny, did you write this absentee note that was supposed to be from your parents?
LENNY: What gave you that idea?
TEACHER: Because it says, "Dear Teacher, Please excuse Lenny for being sick March 30, 31, 32, and 33."

"My son thinks he's a parachute," said Mrs. Stein to the school guidance counselor.
 "Did you try talking to him?" asked the counselor.
 "I tried," said Mrs. Stein, "but he just won't open up."

MORE EXCUSES

From a nutty professor: "On Friday my son will be absent-minded."

From the Invisible Man: "If you don't see my daughter in school this week, it doesn't mean she isn't there."

From a time machine inventor: "My son will not be in school on Friday, but he will show up the previous Tuesday."

From an orchestra conductor: "Please excuse my son as he thinks he's a xylophone. Until he improves, would you please play along with him?"

An old sorceress lay dying in her bed. "Please help me!" she mumbled to her friend, an ugly old crone, then she whispered in the crone's ear.

Jumping onto her broomstick, the crone flew towards the local hospital. Before long, she spotted a physician opening the door of his new Mercedes-Benz. Swooping down, she swiftly plucked the doctor from his car and flew him back to her coven.

"Here's help," said the crone to the sorceress, pointing to the physician.

"No, no!" cried the sorceress, "I said witch doctor, not rich doctor!"

Mother to doctor:
"Does my son have an underactive thyroid?"
"No, just an overactive fork."

Did you hear about the lion that ate a zebra, then had to go the doctor for striped throat?

It was flu vaccination time at school and Perry and his classmates lined up in the cafeteria to get their shots.

When it was Perry's turn, the doctor asked, "Well, son, which arm would you like it in?"

Looking around the room, Perry pointed to the school bully and said, "How about his?"

7. RECESS PIECES

THE KIDS IN MY SCHOOL ARE SO LAZY...

Their school uniforms are pajamas.

Their favorite letters of the alphabet are "Z z z z..."

Their favorite movies are sleepers.

They hire other kids to clean their rooms.

For a field trip, they visited a mattress factory.

At recess one day two boys saw a van suddenly rolling down the parking lot with no one behind the wheel. Quickly they caught up with the vehicle, jumped in and put on the emergency brake. A moment later the door flung open and the principal, his face red with anger, stood staring at them. "What's the big idea?" he asked.

"We stopped this van from getting away," said the first boy.

"I know," said the principal, sweat rolling down his face. "It stalled and I was pushing it."

LANA: What is the difference between peanut butter candies and a torn-up playground?
DANA: One's Reese's Pieces, the other recess pieces.

One day at recess the school bully stopped two boys.

"Give me your lunch money!" growled the bully, "or I'll beat you both up!"

"Whatever you do," said the first boy to the second, "don't give him the $10 you have hidden in your shoe."

WILLIE: Why do you have a postage stamp tattooed to your forehead?
MILLIE: If I get lost I can mail myself home.

Knock-knock!
  Who's there?
Olive.
  Olive who?
Olive recess, don't you?

Why was the pony sent to the principal's office?
For horsing around.

Why do donkeys have a good attendance record?
They get a kick out of class.

The world's cleanest man robbed a bank, then barricaded himself inside his house. Before long the police arrived and surrounded the place.

"Come out with your hands up," shouted one of the officers on the bullhorn, "or we're coming in after you."

After a moment, the man stuck his head out the door and said, "All right, come on in. But be sure you wipe your feet first. I just waxed the floors."

What's half human, half bull, and won't let you into class without a pass?

The Hall Minotaur.

JOE: Last night some crooks robbed our school.
MOE: Did they get a big haul?
JOE: They sure did. In fact, they got the study hall.

How do you know when there's an elephant in the classroom?

Look for the dunce cap with an "E" on it.

NAME DROPPING

WADE: Why do they call you the king of procrastination?
SLADE: I'll tell you later.

MARY: Why does everyone call you "No-Brains"?
GARY: Gee, my mind is a blank.

GERT: Why do all your friends call you "Sparky"?
BERT: I'm shocked to hear they do.

COMPUTER TEACHER: What happened to your laptop?
COMPUTER CLOWN: Some ants crawled inside it.
COMPUTER TEACHER: Well, I hope you work the bugs out.

Our school is so big every classroom has its own zip code.

SAY THESE THREE TIMES QUICKLY

Wayne Watts runs races.

Sheep shouldn't sleep in sheds.

Dolly dilly-dallies daily.

VIDEOS FROM THE NON-FICTION SHELF

Subtraction Magic, hosted by Carry D. Wunn

How to Get Through School Faster,
hosted by Skip A. Yeer

Borrow and Get Rich Quick,
hosted by Allen U. Munny

Communicating with Porpoises,
hosted by Adolph Inne

Understanding Genetics, hosted by Gene Poole

Better Home Security, hosted by Eudora S. Open

8. SHOW @ TAILS

What did the elephant say to the computer?
"Are you a man or a mouse?"

What would you get if you crossed a German shepherd with a jackhammer?
A dog that buries bones in the sidewalk.

What would you get if you crossed a rabbit with a skunk?
Peter Rotten-tail.

There's a squirrel in our neighborhood who has such a bad memory every time he buries a nut he has to draw himself a map.

Show me a hen in a horse race and I'll show you a chicken that lays odds.

What type of fish does not do well in school?
Flounder.

Why did the giraffe graduate early?
She was head and shoulders above the rest.

What's the longest dog in the world?
The 50-yard dachshund.

Knock-knock!
  Who's there?
Roach.
  Roach who?
Roach you a letter, but you never wrote back.

Hank brought his dog to class for show and tell.
Leading the scrawny mutt to the front of the room,
he proudly exclaimed, "This is my dog. He has a
bad case of fleas; he limps from a car accident; he
has worms; and one eye is missing from a fight he
had with a cat."
  "How very nice!" said the teacher. "And what is
your dog's name?"
  "His name's Lucky," replied Hank.

LARRY: Where do fleas go in the wintertime?
BARRY: Search me.

THE WORLD'S WORST WEEVIL RIDDLE

A big weevil and little weevil were crawling along a
path in the forest. Suddenly a hungry anteater came
along, snatched up one of the weevils and ate it.
Which weevil did the anteater choose to eat?
  The lesser of two weevils.

What kind of whale never shuts up?
  A blubbermouth.

What's big and gray and goes, "Crunch! Uh-oh!"?
  An elephant looking for its contact lens.

Sign at animal shelter: "Siamese cat looking for nice home. Honest, reliable, willing to do light mousework."

MUTT: What do you call an octopus convention?
JEFF: 20,000 Legs Under the Sea.

Why did the bees go on strike?
They demanded shorter flowers and more honey.

TEACHER: Why do cows eat green grass?
SHECKY: Because they can't wait for it to ripen.

JUAN: Do smart chickens go to school?
DON: Of course, how else do you think we get Grade A eggs?

What do zebras earn when they do their homework?
Stars and stripes.

WHY THEY'RE MOST LIKELY TO SUCCEED

Fireflies–they're so bright.

Cats–they always get purr-fect scores.

Elephants–they have lots of gray matter.

Porcupines–they're just plain sharp.

Rabbits–they're good at multiplying.

WHY THEY'RE MOST LIKELY TO FAIL

Cows copy off each udder.

Mice barely squeak by.

Squirrels drive the teacher nuts.

Apes monkey around too much.

Lizards keep losing their newt-books.

Turtles are always late for class.

Squids can't ink straight.

Hummingbirds never hand in their hum-work.

Parrots keep repeating their first year.

One day after school Jonathan went to the pet shop and told the owner he wanted to buy a watchdog for his mother's birthday.

"How about this one?" said the salesman, pointing to a cage with a scrawny little poodle in it.

"Are you kidding?" said Jonathan. "That dog looks harmless."

"Yes, but he knows karate," said the salesman. "Watch." The salesman pointed to a huge cinder block and shouted, "Karate the block!"

Immediately, the poodle struck out its paw and with one blow smashed the block into two pieces.

Next, the salesman pointed to a metal chair, then commanded, "Karate the chair!"

Once again, the little poodle crushed the chair with a single blow.

That night Jonathan brought home the poodle and showed it to his father.

"What kind of watchdog is that to give your mother?" said Jonathan's father. "What good is he?"

"But, Dad, this dog knows karate," said Jonathan.

"Oh, come on," said his father. "Karate my foot!"

JON: What is big and gray, has 40 feet, and runs to the post office?
DON: An elephant stamp-ede.

LESTER: What's gray, has a trunk, and is one inch tall?
JESTER: A mouse disguised as an elephant.

What meat-eating dinosaur was made of glass?
Tyrannosaurus Py-Rex.

What caused the shepherd's insomnia?
  Too many sheepless nights.

What dolphin was also a serial killer?
  Jack the Flipper.

What's big and gray and red and blue and yellow
and brown and black?
  An elephant lost in a crayon factory.

Where do frogs keep notes?
  On lily pads.

Where do famous dragons usually end up?
  In the Hall of Flame.

FRIEDA: How do you tell the difference between a dog's answering machine and a cat's?

ANITA: Dogs come when you call them. Cats take a message and get back to you later.

What's dark brown, wears sunglasses, and lives in the Arctic?

A polar bear with a tan.

A woman entered a beauty parlor with a rabbit on her head.

"How can I help you?" asked the beautician, trying not to notice the animal on top of the woman's head.

"Well," said the woman, "you can start by teasing my hare."

TEACHER: What kind of birds are found in the Sahara?

CLASS CLOWN: Hot ones.

Where do whales look up definitions?
In a Moby Dick-tionary.

What's the first thing calves learn in school?
The Alfalfa-bet.

LEM: What would you get if you crossed a best-selling author with an octopus?

CLEM: I don't know, but it could probably autograph eight books at a time.

9. Laugh-A-Teria!

What Wild West hero makes noises when he eats?
Wyatt Slurp.

What is a computer programmer's favorite dessert?
Pie a la modem.

What did the saltcellar say to the pepper mill?
"Let's shake on it!"

First cannibal to second:
"Say, what are these fingers doing in the pizza dough?"
"The recipe said, 'Start with clean hands.'"

DENNY: I think there's nuclear waste in the
  cafeteria.
LENNY: Why do you say that?
DENNY: When I asked for a hamburger the cook
  said, "Is that for here or to glow?

Knock-knock!
  Who's there?
Evan.
  Evan who?

Evan knows what they put in the cafeteria food.

Knock-knock!
  Who's there?
Aida.
  Aida who?
Aida big lunch today!

What did the clock say to the waiter?
  I'll have seconds of everything!"

The food in our school cafeteria is so bad even the
flies have to see the nurse.

Why was the sugar farmer arrested?
  For raising cane.

MOM: Your teacher says you're never first in
  anything.
MITCH: That's not true. I'm always first in line for
  lunch.

How do you prevent break-ins at McDonald's?
With a burger alarm.

SWIFTIES

"This milk is frozen," said Hank icily.

"There's too much pepper on my burger," said Luke hotly.

STACEY: Carrots are good for your eyes.
CASEY: If that's true, how come I see so many dead rabbits on the highway?

The kids at my school are so health-conscious they have basic-food-group fights.

What do boxers eat for lunch?
Open-face sandwiches.

Sign on school bulletin board: "Lost, three weeks ago—lunch bag containing bologna sandwich. If found, please send to biology lab for analysis."

The food in our school cafeteria can't be that bad, because there's always a long line of roaches.

CHRISSY: How would you rank the food in the cafeteria?
MISSY: Why bother? The food's rank already.

JASON: Why did the cannibal go to the Federal Bureau of Investigation for lunch?
MASON: He saw a newspaper headline that said, "FBI Grills Suspect."

What do space aliens toast at campfires?
Mars-mellows.

Why did the police arrest the celery?
For stalking the neighbors.

10. TEACHER FEATURES

A little boy knocked on the door of the teachers' lounge and said, "Did anyone lose $50 attached to a rubber band?"

"Why, yes," said one of the teachers.

"Well, today's your lucky day," said the boy. "I found the rubber band."

TEACHER: What do you want to get out of school the most?

ANDY: Me.

As a police officer directed traffic at a busy intersection, a woman suddenly ran out into the middle of the street.

"Hey," shouted the officer, blowing his whistle, "don't you know what it means when I raise my hand?"

"Of course I do," snapped the woman. "After all, I've been teaching for 30 years!"

Overheard during recess:

"I hear Bobby is no longer teacher's pet."

"What happened?"

"Teacher found out he wasn't housebroken."

"My son is very sensitive," said Mrs. Sommers at a parent-teacher conference.

"Is there anything we should do about it?" asked the teacher.

"Yes," said Mrs. Sommers. "The next time he acts up, punish the boy next to him."

DILLY: Knock-knock!
DALLY: Who's there?
DILLY: Butternut.
DALLY: Butternut who?
DILLY: Butternut talk back to the teacher.

The vice principal asked three contractors to give him an estimate on how much it would cost to fix the school roof.

Ed, the first contractor, carefully surveyed the damaged roof, then jotted down some figures. "It'll cost $900," said Ed to the vice principal. "$400 for materials, $400 for the workers, and $100 for me."

The second contractor, Larry, inspected the roof and wrote down some numbers. "It'll cost $700," said Larry. "$300 for materials, $300 for the workers, and $100 for me."

Finally, the third contractor, Bob, stepped forward and announced, "That'll be $2700!"

"Wait a minute," said the vice principal with a puzzled look on his face. "You didn't even look at the roof. Why is your rate so expensive?"

"It's real simple," said Bob. "$1000 for me, $1000 for you, and we hire the second guy, Larry, for $700."

Art teacher to student:

"What is that a picture of?"

"That's me when I accidentally hammered my finger."

"Oh, it's a self-portrait?"

"No, it's a thumbnail sketch."

Every week for nearly eight months Bruno got sent to the principal's office for getting into some kind of trouble. One day the principal put his foot down and said, "I'm getting tired of seeing you here, Bruno, week after week, day after day. What do you think I should do about it?"

"If you don't like it here," said Bruno, "Why don't you get transferred to another school?"

MOM: Did teacher call on you in class today?
TINA: Well, she tried, but my cell phone was busy.

TEACHER: Henry, if you want to learn anything, you
   have to start at the bottom.
HENRY: Yes, but I want to be an oceanographer.

What part of the computer patrols the school
corridors?
   The Hall Monitor.

COMPUTER TEACHER: Emily, why does your Apple
   computer have teeth marks on it?
EMILY: I think someone took a few bytes out of it.

What did the principal do when he found out the
weight machine was stolen from the nurse's office?
   He launched a full-scale investigation.

Why did the principal expel the polka-dotted
elephant?
   For violating the dress code.

SILLY CLOTHING INVENTION

Turtleskin shoes. They look nice, but wherever
you go you're always two hours late.

TEACHER: What happens when salmon return to
   their place of birth?
CLASS CLOWN: All the other salmon sing, "Happy
birthday!"

TEACHER: Name two ranges.
CLASS CLOWN: Gas and electric.

TEACHER: Cindy, would you take a note to your mother?
CINDY: Sure, how about a B-flat?

When Principal Skinner's wife passed away he had her cremated and her ashes placed in an urn on the coffee table. For several days afterwards, Principal Skinner's friends, all of whom were heavy smokers, came to visit and pay their respects.

One day the principal's mother came to call. She took one look at the urn and said, "Son, I hate to tell you this, but I think your wife is gaining weight."

MOM: How was the first day of school?
TONY: The teacher showed a video; then everyone stood up and walked out.
MOM: Why did they do that?
TONY: Because the video was over.

11. SOME ASSEMBLY REQUIRED

Why did the comb take acting lessons?
To get a good part.

SCHOOL JEOPARDY

ANSWER: Razorbill.
QUESTION: What does the doctor do when you can't pay for your checkup?

As she passed her son's room one night, Hank's mother heard a booming voice cry out, "To be or not to be! That is the question."

"Hank!" said his mother, knocking on the door. "What are you doing in there?"

"Exactly what you told me to," said Hank. "You said I should stay in my room until I learn how to act."

Twelve-year-old Joey went to the movies, but they wouldn't let him in because a sign said, "Under 17 not allowed." So Joey went home and brought back 16 of his friends.

"What did you think of the magician at the assembly?" the teacher asked Philip.

"He wasn't very good," replied Philip. "But the teacher he sawed in half was terrific!"

What game do classical composers play?
Haydn Seek.

"What will you do in the school talent show?"
  "My imitation of the Invisible Man."
  "That should be impressive."
  "Are you kidding? You ain't seen nothing yet!"

"What are you going to do in the school talent show?"
  "My imitation of a bird."
  "What do you have planned?"
  "Nothing, I'm just going to wing it."

YOU KNOW IT'S GOING TO BE A BAD DAY WHEN...

...all you get on Valentine's Day is a card addressed "Occupant."

...your alphabet soup spells out "Stupid."

...you find out you're an underachiever and your teacher is an overexpecter.

...opportunity knocks at your door, you're busy mowing the lawn.

...you go to a palm reader and she can't find your life line.

...you drop your open-faced peanut-butter-and-jelly sandwich and it lands jelly-side-down.

...your VCR breaks down the same day you win a video-club membership.

...you have to pay overdue fines at the library for *How to Improve Your Memory*.

12. HISTORIC HYSTERICS

TEACHER: Give an example of a national disaster.
CLOWN: How about my last report card?

How did the famous pirate introduce himself?
   "I Kidd, you not!"

How did Attila's wife greet him when he came home?
   "How was your day, Hun?"

Dragon Slayer's motto: "No slain, no gain."

What did Dracula say when he saw the vampire hunter?

"Now there's a man after my own heart."

One day Lenny bragged to his friend Vinny that he was personally acquainted with some of the most famous people in the world.

"I'm a good friend of Steven Spielberg's," bragged Lenny.

"Prove it," said Vinny. "Let's see you call him on the phone."

A few minutes later Lenny was at a pay phone dialing a number. After a moment, Lenny handed the phone to Vinny as a voice on the other end said, "Hello, this is Steven Spielberg."

"That was just a trick," said Vinny. "Next you're gonna tell me you know the Queen of England."

Once again, Lenny dialed a number and gave the phone to Vinny. "Hello, the Queen of England speaking!"

"I still don't believe you," said Vinny.

That night the President of the United States came to town to give a speech. Lenny and Vinny arrived early to get a seat, but the moment the President was introduced, Lenny disappeared. Vinny couldn't believe his eyes when he saw his friend on stage shaking hands with the leader of the country.

Suddenly the woman seated next to Vinny nudged his shoulder and asked, "Hey, who's that guy on the stage shaking hands with Lenny?"

WHOEVER INVENTED...?

Whoever invented sandpaper must have had a rough time.

Whoever invented the automobile must have had a strong drive.

Whoever invented the elevator must have had a lot of ups and downs.

Book title: *The Man Who Invented Everything,*
by Pat N. Pending

Tim's absent-minded father was reminiscing about his youth. "When I was your age," he said proudly, "I had to walk 10 miles through the snow to get to school."

"Was it really that far?" asked Tim.

"Not really," said Tim's father, scratching his head. "It was right across the street, but I was terrible at directions."

Who was the world's greatest owl magician?
Whoooo-dini.

What would you get if you crossed a small bus with a famous painter?
Mini-Van Gogh.

What did the famous composer say when he bent over to tie his shoe?
"Oh my aching Bach."

TEACHER: Why did William Tell shoot an apple off his son's head?
CLASS CLOWN: Because he couldn't find an IBM.

Which of Robin Hood's men was always falling apart?
Brittle John.

Where in the U.S. Constitution does it mention that you can wear sleeveless shirts?
The part where it says, "the right to bear arms."

MELENA: What occurs once in a century, twice in a lifetime, but not even once in a day?
SELENA: The letter "e."

ZIP: Knock-knock!
ZAP: Who's there?
ZIP: Goliath.
ZAP: Goliath who?
ZIP: Goliath down and take a nap.

TEACHER: What can you tell us about the Iron Age?
MELVIN: Sorry, but I'm a bit rusty on that topic.

LES: Where in Egypt can you get help for your bad
    back?
WES: At the Cairo-practor.

CLINT: What biblical story tells about a dentist who
    pulls his brother's tooth?
FLINT: Novocaine and Abel.

RONNY: Where did Noah keep all his important papers?
JOHNNY: In his Ark-ives.

Which of Robin Hood's men made sure everyone got to bed on time?
Friar Tuck-Me-In.

What was Brachiosaurus' favorite vegetable?
Squash.

DANA: In what period of time did the dinosaur Sloppy-a-saurus live?
LANA: During the Messy-zoic period, of course.

TEACHER: What is your class report on?
HANK: The history of underwear.
TEACHER: Will it be long?
HANK: No, it'll be brief.

MOM: How did you manage to flunk history?
NICKY: Because everything the teacher says goes in both ears and out the other.
MOM: But that's three ears!
NICKY: I'm not doing well in math, either.

13. HOME, WORK & PLAY

PORKY!... I WANT YOUR ESSAY CHOP CHOP!

HOMEWORK HOWLERS

TEACHER: For homework I want you to write a paper on pigs.

CLOWN: Is it okay if I use invisible oink?

HAROLD: Teacher, would you punish me for not capitalizing letters on my homework?

TEACHER: No, I'd just mark you down.

HAROLD: Oh, I didn't think you believed in capital punishment.

FRIEDA: I have a new baby sister.
ANITA: What's her name?
FRIEDA: I keep asking, but she won't tell me.

Henry was the world's worst oversleeper. One day, fearing that he may have overslept again, Henry jumped out of bed, dressed, and ran outside just as the school bus pulled up in front of his house.

"I made it, didn't I?" sighed Henry as the door flew open.

"I don't think so," said the bus driver, then shouted, "Day's over! Everybody off!"

One night two burglars broke into a house. As they climbed through a window, they suddenly heard the sound of loud voices arguing upstairs.

"Wait a second," said the first robber, "we can't rob this family."

"But why not?" said the second robber.

"Because," said the first robber, all choked up, "it sounds too much like home."

Knock-knock!
  Who's there?
Canal.
  Canal who?
Canal come out and play with me?

Christmas at our shopping mall is so busy they have two lines to see Santa Claus—one for lots of toys and an express line for 10 toys or less.

HOMEWORK EXCUSES

1) After I finished my paper on the importance of recycling, I decided to do my part by recycling it.

2) I put it in my locker, but somebody jammed it with bubble gum and I can't get it open.

3) I was on an ocean liner and it sprung a leak. I plugged the hole with my homework and saved hundreds of lives.

4) I did my report on the history of hamburger and it was so good my little brother ate it.

5) My sister put it on the bottom of her parakeet cage.

6) My uncle built a time machine and took it with him. You should have gotten it three years ago.

7) I got it mixed up with the homework from last week that I forgot to do, so I did the wrong assignment.

8) My mom brought home our new baby sister from the hospital and she didn't have any diapers, so...

9) The paper is blank because I used invisible ink.

10) I was kidnapped and my dad used it for ransom.

MOM: Why were you expelled from school?
TOM: I used a hose to fill up the swimming pool.
MOM: I didn't know your school had a pool?
TOM: It does now.

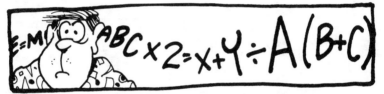

Notice on bulletin board: "There will be a meeting of the Mind Readers Club at...well, you know what time."

"Mom, is it true that on the day I was born, the mailman brought me?"
   "Yes, it was a special delivery."

Father to son watching TV:
"Theodore, when I was your age things were a lot different."
   "How were they different, Dad?"
   "Well, for one thing, I had to walk all the way across the room to change the channel."

14. HI-TECH TICKLES

What do you call a computer that's mean and grouchy?

A Crab Apple.

What kind of computer would you find in the Garden of Eden?

Adam's Apple.

What did the computer programmer say to the waiter?

"May I see a pull down menu?"

Wise man says, "If you drop a computer, let the chips fall where they may."

MADDIE: How do you stop a computer from running away from home?
PATTIE: Unplug it.

LORIE: Which thinks faster, a computer or a human being?
DORIE: Uh, can I get back to you on that one?

STAN: Our new car is completely computerized.
DAN: Hard drive?
STAN: No, actually it's easy to drive.

JOE: We have a new software program at our house that cooks, washes, and puts us to bed.
MOE: What's it called?
JOE: CD-MOM.

SILLY SOFTWARE

Did you hear about the new software program for male cats? It's called CD-TOM.

Did you hear about the new software program for terrorists? It's called CD-BOMB.

Did you hear about the new software program for high-school seniors? It's called CD-PROM.

Did you hear about the new software program for teaching the alphabet? It's called ABCD-ROM.

Why did the computer go to the hospital?
It caught a bug.

Why don't computers drive cars?
Because they're always crashing.

Computer programmer's motto: "P.C. come, P.C. go."

Computer homework excuse: "The hard drive ate my homework."

GINNY: Did you hear about the crooks who built their own automatic teller machine?
VINNY: It dispenses counterfeit bills.

QUICK CASH QUIP

What machine dispenses money at gun shops?
A semi-automatic teller machine.

RONNY: What's a cat's favorite type of computer?
DONNY: A laptop.

Why did Godzilla smash the computer?
He wanted Apple sauce.

A computer technician was called to an office to repair a computer. Unable to find a parking spot, the repairman left his car in a no-parking zone with a note on the windshield saying, "Bob Smith, computer technician, working inside the building."

Later, when he returned to his car, he found a ticket and a note on his windshield saying, "Joe Thompson, police officer, working outside the building."

Sign at computer cafeteria: "Stop in and have a byte."

GENE: Do computers like people?
IRENE: Of course. Who do you think turn them on?

15. SILLY SCIENCE & JOLLY GEOGRAPHY

TEACHER: Danny, when is the boiling point reached?

DANNY: Usually, when my father sees my report card.

TEACHER: Joey, how fast does sound travel?

JOEY: I'm sorry, I didn't catch what you said.

One day in biology lab an absent-minded professor said to his students, "Today, we will dissect a frog and see what it's made of."

Placing a bag on the table, he reached in and pulled out a peanut-butter sandwich. Scratching his head, he sighed and said, "That's funny. I distinctly remember eating my lunch earlier today!"

Where do biologists like to swim?
In the gene pool.

TEACHER: Bobby, can you date this rock?
BOBBY: Are you kidding? My mom says I'm too young to date.

What's big and gray and goes, "Bubble, bubble, ka-boom!"
An elephant experimenting with a chemistry set.

What's big and gray and lives in a beaker?
A test-tube elephant.

What did the astronaut say when he couldn't solve the math equation?
"Houston, we have a problem!"

What do you call a Radio City showgirl who works for NASA?
A Rock-ette scientist.

NURSE: Doctor, the time traveler is here to see you.
DOCTOR: Tell him to come back yesterday.

THE WORLD'S WORST CLONE JOKE

One day a mad scientist cloned himself. The clone was perfect in every way, except for one thing–the clone wouldn't stop cursing. Unable to take it any longer, the mad scientist decided to get rid of his foul-mouthed friend once and for all. The next day while hiking with his clone, the mad scientist pushed him off the edge of a cliff.

The following day, the police arrived at the laboratory and slapped handcuffs on the scientist.

"Wait a minute," the scientist protested, "what am I being arrested for?"

"Isn't it obvious?" said one of the police officers. "You're charged with making an obscene clone fall."

CRAZY CLONES

"Do you want to be cloned?"
  "Why tamper with perfection?"

"You should clone your hair."
  "Who wants split ends?"

"Would you rather be cloned or be invisible?"
  "Sounds like double or nothing to me."

Who cracks jokes in science lab?
  The class clone.

What did the science teacher say to the twin
biology students?
  "Stop cloning around."

First Martian: Why did you put a blanket over
  our flying saucer?
Second Martian: It isn't just a blanket, it's a UFO
  cover-up.

Two extra-terrestrials watched as astronauts
scooped up some rocks from the moon's surface,
then got back in their space shuttle and blasted off
for Earth. When the astronauts were gone, one
creature said to the other, "Well, there goes the
garden."

Who led the parade in space?
  A Martian band.

Did you hear about the Martians who got married on Saturn? It was a double-ring ceremony.

What is an astronaut's favorite section of the newspaper?
The orbit-uaries.

What did the rocket scientist say to the missile?
"You're fired!"

What do computerized parrots say?
"Polly want a hacker."

What did the boy robot get for Christmas?
A trans-sister.

SPACE RIDDLE

An astronaut in the space shuttle tried to take a picture of the Earth from outer space, but it turned out blurry. Why?
Someone moved.

16 AFTER-SCHOOL CRACK-UPS

One night after his parents had gone to bed, Freddy picked up the phone and dialed the Psychic Hotline.

"Hello," said a woman's voice, "who's calling?"

"You're the psychic," said Freddy. "Why don't you tell me?"

What keeps dolls from escaping?
Barbie wire.

DID YOU HEAR ABOUT?

Did you hear about the slime monster who was a born oozer?

Did you hear about the fisherman who carried a cell phone, but his line was always busy?

Did you hear about the ballerina who wanted a job that kept her on her toes?

Did you hear about the paleontologist who dug her job?

How do you mail a jet?
In a plane brown wrapper.

What action figures do farmers' sons play with?
G-I-E-I-Joe.

What would you get if you crossed Sir Lancelot with a zombie?
Knight of the Living Dead.

SAY THESE THREE TIMES QUICKLY

Six sneaky sharks shouted sharply.

Frieda fries fresh fish on Fridays.

Steve saves shoes, shells, and shamrocks.

What did the hypnotist say to the girl at the high school dance?
"May I have this trance?"

SUNDAY SCHOOL TEACHER: Do you want to go straight to heaven?
SUNDAY SCHOOL PUPIL: No, ma'am, my mother said I have to go straight home.

Two police officers stopped a young boy on the street and said, "We're looking for a kidnapper with a baby carriage."
"Wouldn't it be quicker to use a squad car instead?"

Lenny: Did you like my joke about the postcard that had no stamp on it?
Benny: I didn't get it.
Lenny: And you never will.

Knock-knock!
  Who's there?
Manuel.
  Manuel who?
Manuel be sorry if you don't clean your room.

When school finally let out for summer vacation, one teacher said to another, "Boy, you should have heard the excitement. When the bell rang, everyone stomped their feet and shouted for joy!"

"It was pretty wild, huh?" remarked the second teacher.

"You bet it was!" replied the first. "And that was just in the teacher's lounge!"

ODE TO THE LAST DAY

Roses are red,
Cacti are prickly,
Summer vacation
Better come quickly.

FIRST STUDENT: Did you notice how on the last day of school, every student turns into a magician?
SECOND STUDENT: That's because we know how to disappear for the summer!

About the Authors

Matt and Philip are graduates of the school of hard knock-knocks. Their other books include *World's Silliest Jokes, The Great Book of Zany Jokes,* and the *Biggest Joke Book in the World,* also published by Sterling. They have performed at schools, libraries, and hospitals for children. Matt lives near Valley Forge, Pennsylvania, with his wife, Maggie, and daughters, Rebecca, Emily, and Abigail. Philip makes his home in Austin, Texas, with Maria and their two cats, Sam and Johnnie.

About the Illustrator

Jeff Sinclair has been drawing cartoons ever since he could hold a pen. He has won several local and national awards for cartooning and humorous illustration. When he is not at his drawing board, he can be found renovating his house and working on a water garden in the backyard. He lives in Vancouver, British Columbia, Canada, with his wife, Karen, son, Brennan, daughter, Conner, and golden Lab, Molly.

Gill Memorial Library
Broad and Commerce
Paulsboro, NJ   08066
(609) 423-5155

GAYLORD